Disney and Disney/Pixar characters
and artwork © Disney Enterprises, Inc.

ISBN 978-1-4234-8411-0

WALT DISNEY MUSIC COMPANY

DISTRIBUTED BY

HAL•LEONARD®
CORPORATION

7777 W. BLUEMOUND RD. P.O. BOX 13819 MILWAUKEE, WI 53213

In Australia Contact:
Hal Leonard Australia Pty. Ltd.
4 Lentara Court
Cheltenham, Victoria, 3192 Australia
Email: ausadmin@halleonard.com.au

Visit Hal Leonard Online at
www.halleonard.com

UP WITH TITLES

By MICHAEL GIACCHINO

Moderately fast, in 2

MARRIED LIFE

By MICHAEL GIACCHINO

Moderately fast

Slightly faster

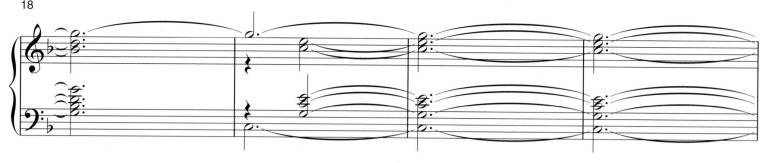

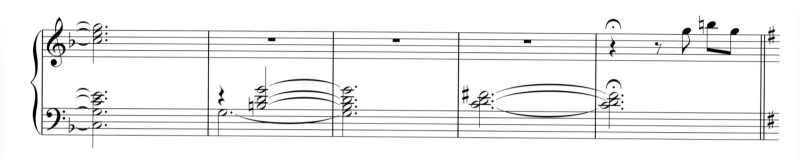

WE'RE IN THE CLUB NOW

By MICHAEL GACCHINO

Moderately slow

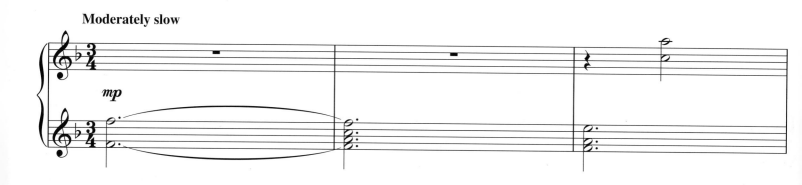

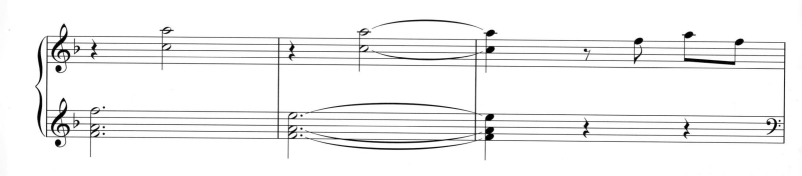

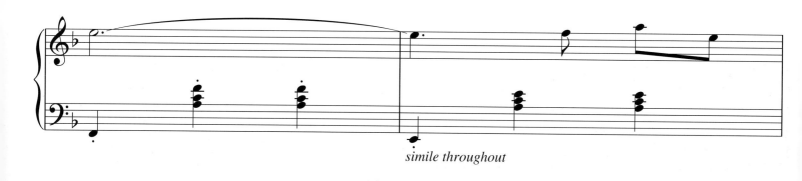

simile throughout

CARL GOES UP

By MICHAEL GIACCHINO

Moderately

Pedal ad lib. throughout

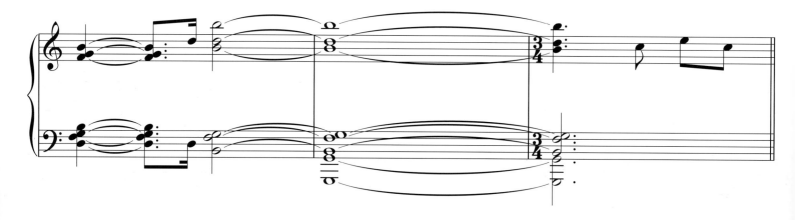

Lilting waltz

PARADISE FOUND

By MICHAEL GIACCHINO

KEVIN BEAK'N

By MICHAEL GIACCHINO

Moderate Latin beat

STUFF WE DID

By MICHAEL GIACCHINO

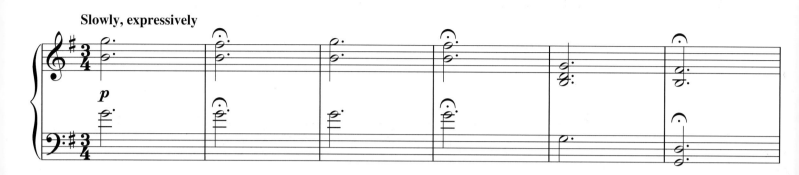

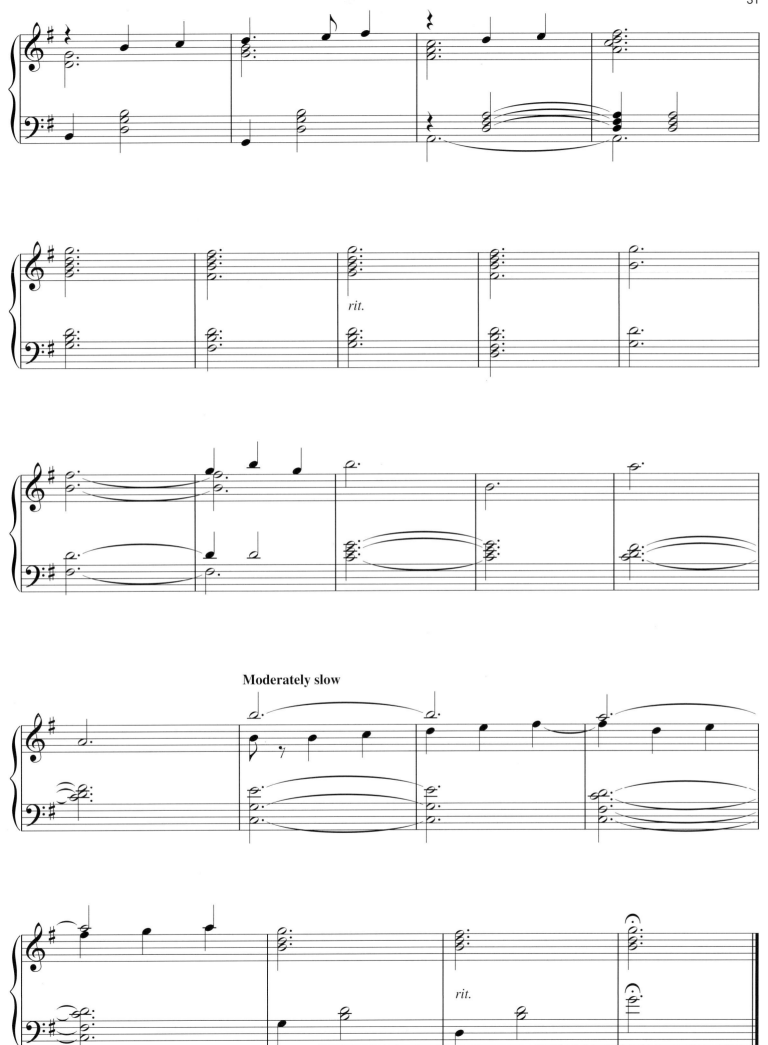

THE NICKEL TOUR

By MICHAEL GIACCHINO

Moderately slow, expressively

Pedal ad lib.

MEMORIES CAN WEIGH YOU DOWN

By MICHAEL GIACCHINO

Brisk March

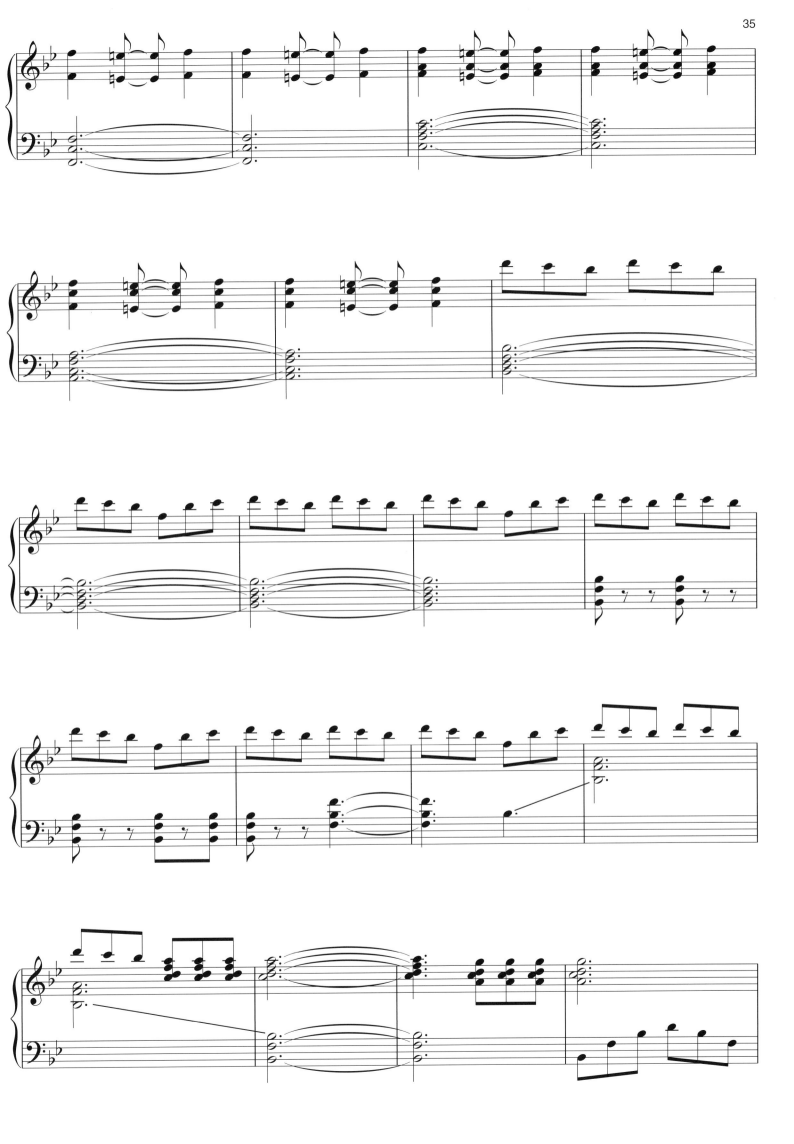

THE SMALL MAILMAN RETURNS

By MICHAEL GIACCHINO

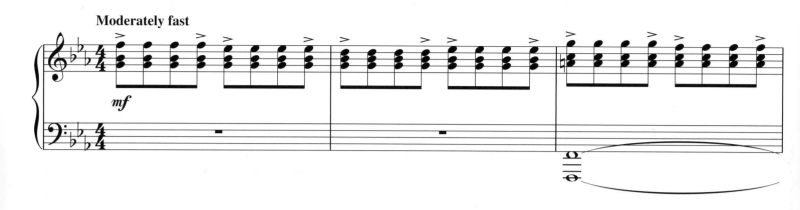

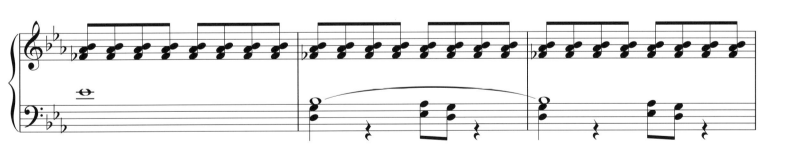

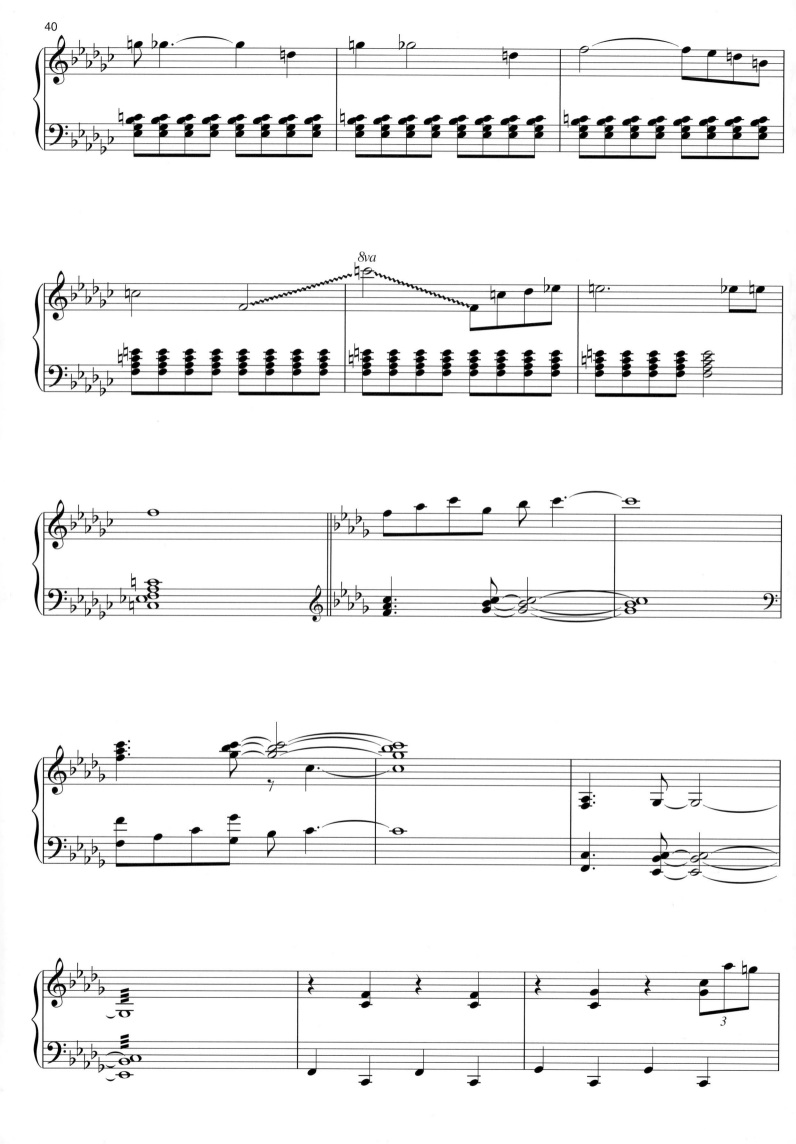

IT'S JUST A HOUSE

By MICHAEL GIACCHINO

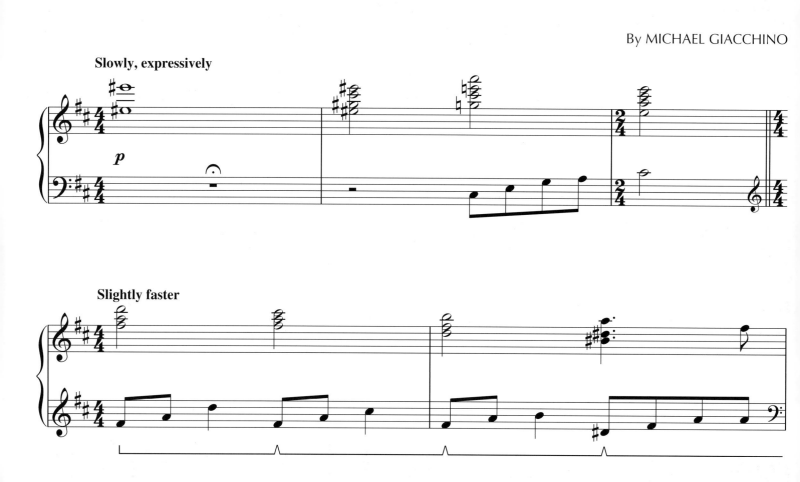

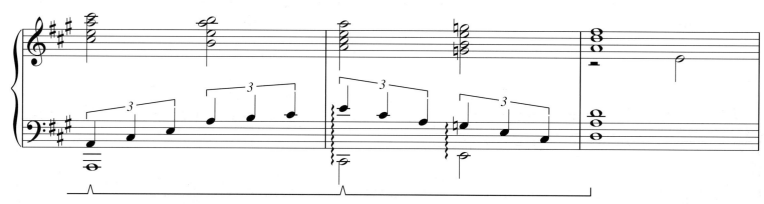

UP WITH END CREDITS

By MICHAEL GIACCHINO

Moderately fast waltz

THE SPIRIT OF ADVENTURE

Words and Music by
MICHAEL GIACCHINO